Crossing the street

MB MACAW BOOKS

www.macawbooks.com

Printed in India

Billy and Mummy were out on a trip to the town. How excited he was! Mummy had promised to take him to the candy store. "i will eat all the candy in the shop!' said Billy, happily.

Candy Shop

Soon they reached the candy store. But it was on the other side of the street.

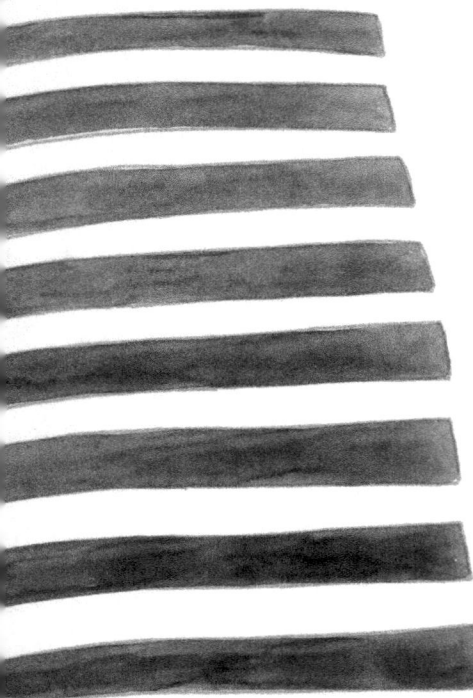

'We shall have to walk to the other side to reach the store,' said Mummy, 'Do you remember the traffic rules, darling?'

'Yes, I do, Mummy!' said Billy. The traffic light was green at the moment. 'When the light turns red, then the cars will stop. Then we can cross the street safely!' said Billy. And so they waited for the light to turn red.

The colour of the traffic light was green. That meant go for the cars and buses. So Billy and his Mummy waited for the vehicles to pass.

The yellow light meant it was time to wait for the cars to go. So he waited for the cars to go, and the traffic slowed down.

When the light turned red, all the cars stopped. It was time for Billy and his Mummy to cross! Billy remembered to look left, and then to look right. Then they safely crossed the street.

Billy walked calmly on the zebra crossing. He was not nervous. He did not run, or hop. Mummy was so proud of him! She bought Billy a lot of yummy candy at the store.

After reaching the other side, Billy ate yummy candy at the store. Later Mummy and Billy went to the toy store too. What a fun day they had at the town!

Fire
safety

One afternoon, Tessie was at home alone. She was reading quietly when she heard a bell ringing.

'Tring ting! Tring tring!' it rang. It was the fire alarm!

When the fire alarm rang, it meant that there was a fire in the house. It started with a spark in an electrical wire.

Then the spark became
bigger, until the
curtains were on fire!
'How do I put out the
fire?' thought Tessie.

Just then, the water sprinklers came on. Fat drops of water rained down on the fire. But the fire did not stop burning. Instead, it began to spread.

The house was filling up with smoke! Tessie could not see too well anymore. Her eyes began to burn.

Fire exit

If she stayed in the house, she would choke or faint. She ran out of the house as fast as she could.

Tessie found her way to the fire exit of her building. She climbed down the stairs of the escape route. Soon she was outside the house. She ran out to the neighbourhood and shouted for help.

Tessie rushed to a clear and safe place, and shouted, 'Help! There is a fire in my house! Somebody please help!' Two adults were walking past the house. They heard Tessie and called the fire department to put out the fire.

Soon the fire engine arrived.
Tessie was so relieved! Many brave
firemen ran out of the vehicle.

They brought with them long
ladders and hose pipes full of water.
The firemen quickly put the fire out.

When the house was safe, and the fire was out, the fireman said, 'You have been very brave, Tessie!' Tessie was very proud of herself too.